The Ach

Thru-Hiking the Colorado Trail

Jim (Simba) Rahtz

ISBN-13:
978-1502545435

ISBN-10:
1502545438

“Table of Contents”

Chapter 1: Decisions, Decisions..5

Chapter 2: Yea, I Hiked (on) the Appalachian Trail 10

Chapter 3: The Plan...16

Chapter 4: Getting Physical..20

Chapter 5: Limping onto the Trail 22

Chapter 6: The Weight..27

Chapter 7: Reality begins 29

Chapter 8: Up to the Divide 35

Chapter 9: Frisco 39

Chapter 10: Snow in July..44

Chapter 11: Getting a Little Company..48

Chapter 12: Wishing...51

Chapter 13: Prediction? Pain 55

Chapter 14: Closing in on Halfway 58

Chapter 15: A Family is Born..61

Chapter 16: Cow Country...65

Chapter 17: Lake City 70

Chapter 18: Onto the High Ground..73

Chapter 19: Walking the Great Divide 76

Chapter 20: Into Silverton..79

Chapter 21: The Final Stretch...82

Chapter 22: More Punishment 87

Chapter 23: How About It? 90

Chapter 24: My Gear..93

Final Travel Detail 99

Acknowledgements..104

Chapter 1: Decisions, Decisions…

Starting down from the Continental Divide, the trail curved away from its southern exposure and the snow began to deepen. Before long, the three of us were alternating between climbing up and over crusty ridges of ice and dropping crotch deep into the snow, or post holing.

After a mile or so, we were exhausted and stopped for lunch. Wildflower sat against a tree and I noticed a good size gash in her leg. As she mopped up the blood she talked about how her "country club" friends didn't understand why she liked backpacking so much. "That's true," I remarked, "Some people just don't appreciate how much fun it is to be laying in the snow….on the side of a mountain… bleeding."

Perhaps fun wasn't the best word to describe our situation. Despite the hardship however, or maybe because of it, thru-hiking the Colorado Trail turned out to be one of the most rewarding experiences I have ever had.

I'm in my mid-fifties, retired after a career in Parks and Recreation Management. Working part time as a zip line guide, participating in running races and triathlons and traveling wasn't quite working out as the challenge I needed to be satisfied with my life. After being re-introduced to backpacking by an old friend, I started to consider a long distance backpacking trip as a tonic for the empty feeling I was dealing with. But which trail would I attempt?

If you've ever backpacked at all, you've probably thought about hiking the most famous long distance hiking trail in the world, the Appalachian Trail, or AT. Of course, that thought might have been, "no way in hell," but you thought about it nonetheless. I've thought about attempting that one as well. I've even gone so far as to do a little research on what hiking the AT would entail. Beyond a little Internet study I've read some books about hiking the trail. As of this writing, my Kindle contains 24 books written by successful AT thru-hikers.

Luckily for you, there is no need to read that many books. While the writing styles and abilities vary considerably, the information in the books is surprisingly consistent. Nearly every book makes the same main points. Here's my take on every book ever written about the AT.

1. The author was woefully unprepared for the rigors encountered.

2. The hiking was much more difficult than imagined.

3. The shelters were often crowded, dirty and full of mice.

4. Privies along the way can be nasty.

5. It rained.... A lot. Plan on being wet for days at a time.

6. At times, the mosquitoes or other bugs were unrelenting.

7. There's a significant chance you'll get Lyme disease and/or West Nile disease.

8. There are some amazing views, but much of the time you're hiking in a "green tunnel."

9. Six months of hiking can get surprisingly difficult on a psychological basis; also difficult on any relationships back home.

10. There will be tough times when it takes tremendous willpower to keep from quitting.

11. It was a wonderful experience.

And these are people that finished. Other than Bill Bryson's A Walk in the Woods, not many books have been written by those that didn't finish the trail. You have to wonder if their viewpoint would tilt more towards negativity.

As an alternative to what was starting to appear to me to be a 2,000 mile plus slog, I began looking at the Colorado Trail; 500 miles through the Rocky Mountains from Denver to Durango. For me, at least while I was sitting in my warm, dry house, the Colorado Trail (CT) offered the challenges and benefits of a long distance hike while avoiding some of the hardships and drawbacks of the AT.

1. Only about 150 people attempt the CT each year (compared to 3,000 on the AT), so crowds on the trail or at prime camp areas should be non-existent. (Downside – Don't get hurt; you may be on your own. Fix that snapped femur with duct tape and a stick. You did bring duct tape, didn't you?)

2. There are no shelters to be disappointed in. (Downside – There's no shelters to use for things like…..shelter. When it rains, you're getting wet.)

3. There are no privies to be disappointed in. (Bonus – your leg muscles will get stronger from squatting.)

4. Less rain and bugs. (Hard to find a downside there, other than it may snow instead.)

5. The highest point on the AT is Clingman's Dome at 6,625 feet. The average elevation of the CT is over 10,000 feet. You'll spend significant time above tree line with amazing views nearly every day. (Downside – There's a lot less oxygen up there. At its high point, 13,271 feet, there's nearly 40% less air than at sea level. Also, when it does rain/snow that high in the summer, there's typically lightning and you're the tallest thing around.)

6. The Colorado Trail can be done in 5 weeks. A long hike to be sure, but short enough to see light at the end of the tunnel during a bad day. (Assuming the bad day isn't Day 2.) Of course, that's still plenty of time to see how I would look with a neck beard. Plus, at my age, a month or so may even be enough time to grow a nice crop of ear hair. I'd have to wait and see on that one.

7. It seemed like there would be plenty of challenge and adventure. The trail crosses eight mountain ranges, travels through six wilderness areas and is known, at least in the

trail's guidebook, as the "most beautiful long trail in the world."

And, it would be hard to beat singing John Denver songs like "I Guess He'd Rather be in Colorado" as I hike in the Rockies; provided I could suck in enough air to do anything beyond panting and wheezing.

While it appeared the decision had been made, I thought a test hike on the AT would be a good idea; just to double-check my judgment.

Chapter 2: Yea, I Hiked (on) the Appalachian Trail

Approximately 3,000 people attempt to thru-hike the Appalachian Trail (AT) in any given year. Generally, only about a quarter of those actually finish the 2,100 + mile hike from Georgia to Maine (or vice versa). About the same percentage give up by the time they reach Neel Gap, just over 30 miles from the southern starting point and home of the famous Mountain Crossings Outfitter. The reasons they quit are many, but often center on being poorly prepared, poorly equipped, or the hike "just isn't fun anymore."

The experienced staff at Mountain Crossings has saved many a thru-hiker by way of their pack "shakedown service." Hikers that stagger the first 2-4 days from Springer Mountain with packs full of unneeded (like jars of mayonnaise) or overly heavy items (iron skillets) can get a new lease on their hike's life when a successful thru-hiker goes through their load; getting rid of all non-essentials and selling replacements for poorly chosen gear. Each year, Mountain Crossings helps ship literally thousands of pounds of extra gear back to hiker's homes while the hikers themselves continue north with a significantly lighter pack (and wallet).

As I was considering a thru-hike, I thought a test run on an early section of the AT would be a prudent idea. Rather than possibly carry extra weight for any length of time, I thought I'd start my hike at Mountain Crossings. Packed for 4 days of late fall weather, I gave my 32 pound pack to Squirrel (not his given name) for inspection.

With the gear being fairly lightweight, Squirrel didn't find a tremendous amount of weight savings. Rather than carry a 1.2 ounce fleece pillow cover, he pointed out that the hood on my rain jacket could be stuffed with extra clothes to make a nice rubbery pillow. Nothing lulls you to sleep like laying your face down on coated nylon. Squirrel thought he hit the mother lode of savings in the toiletries when he spotted a mirror. When I stated that I needed it to put in my contact lenses, Squirrel suggested Lasik as a weight saving technique. Unfortunately, none of the staff there were prepared to perform the procedure on me that day, so I was stuck with the weight. He also pointed out that my 12 ounce Kindle was a "luxury" item. However, between camping alone and over 14 hours of darkness each night, it stayed in the "essential" pile.

Squirrel did provide some excellent advice on packing. By splitting up my tent poles and body, the body could be compressed into a smaller size. In addition, with a new waterproof compression sack purchased for my sleeping bag, he shrunk it from the size of a volleyball down closer to the size of a baseball. Pretty impressive, especially if I'm able to ever get the bag back into the compression sack. Squirrel also recommended the purchase of a new pack rain cover.

Although I was carrying the lightest option for water purification, pills, Squirrel enticed me with a new, lightweight water filter. Water could be rendered safe much quicker than the pills, and with the add-on straw feature, I could drink straight out of a mud puddle if so desired. Sold! I finished the "shakedown" with my pack a few ounces heavier than when I arrived, but my wallet $100 lighter.

When the time came to stash my car at the parking lot ½ mile away, I received my first "trail magic." Squirrel's co-worker (Chipmunk?) offered to meet there and drive me back to Mountain Crossings to begin the hike without needing to walk along the road; a great start.

The day was cool, but sunny. Heading out the back of the outfitters, I followed a trail winding up the mountain, eager to start following the white blazes that would lead me as far as I wanted to go; all the way to Maine if I decided to. Fifteen minutes later, eagerness was being replaced with apprehension as I had yet to see my first blaze. This certainly wasn't what I was used to. At Zaleski State Forest in Ohio, there are spots where the markings are thick enough to see the next six blazes at one time. After seeing one faded blaze in the first half hour, I broke down and checked the location on my phone's AT app. (Yes, there's an app for that.) It only took half the available battery supply to pinpoint it, but my location was indeed on the AT, and going in the proper direction.

The trail itself is rocky and regularly contains root tripping hazards. Since it was late November though, the perils were nicely covered by a blanket of fallen leaves; safely out of sight and out of mind. Once up on the first mountain though, the views were absolutely amazing.

The topography was a bit different than Ohio as well. Guidebooks for Buckeye backpack trails describe 300 foot elevation changes as grim, epic or lung busters. In this area of the AT, it is not unusual, in a bit over two miles, to climb 1,000 feet, drop back down 1,000 feet, and be looking at another 1,000+ foot climb. A great workout for the calves.

A few miles into the hike I ran into a southbound thru-hiker. Weed n Feed was stopped for a snack with his dog, Blunt. His favorite part of the trail was the Grayson Highlands of Virginia, where there are wild horses living along the trail. He had a visible reaction when I asked about mosquitoes during the summer. His action plan during one stretch was to never stop walking during the day and immediately set up his tent when reaching a camp area. He'd then spend the rest of his waking hours in the tent, even cooking by just sticking a hand outside to operate his stove. It sounded less than fun.

By late afternoon the wind had picked up and the temperature was dropping. I made Low Gap Shelter with about an hour of daylight left. I left my pack on the picnic table and quickly set up my tent. No mud puddles were to be found, so the filtered water had to come from a nearby clear creek. Once back to the pack to start dinner, I noticed a mouse had beaten me there, chewing through my food bag and a Ziploc bag to help himself to some of my trail mix. Great. The remaining undamaged food was hung up in the trees for the evening.

By the time dinner, a lovely entrée of freeze dried chili that bore a striking resemblance to Alpo, was finished, the sun was down. Being as it was cold, dark and too windy for a fire, I retired to the tent with my Kindle and a flask. It was 6 PM. The flask was to last three nights, so there was some tough rationing ahead.

At 9 PM the flask was empty. The Kindle became my sole entertainment. To stay in the hiking mood, the tablet was loaded with several books written by thru-hikers. Reading one book, I absorbed page after page of despair caused by hiking through continuous rain and flooding. It must have been extraordinarily tiring. I know I got tired of reading about it. Eventually, the warmth of the sleeping bag and the white noise of the wind (and possibly the contents of the flask) lulled me to sleep.

After a full night's sleep, I lay in the tent, waiting for daylight when I heard the first drops of rain. As I crawled out of the tent at dawn, a hard rain was falling and a heavy, cold fog had moved in, reducing visibility to about 50 feet.

Stuffing my wet gear into the pack I thought, “This isn’t fun anymore.” I wonder, could you spot those wild horses from a car?

The decision was made. If I was going to thru-hike a trail, it wasn’t going to be the AT. So, Colorado Trail it would be.

Chapter 3: The Plan

If I was going to hike 500 miles, solo, through the Rocky Mountains; I figured I should probably come up with a plan. An Internet search provided some information and a few first person accounts of the hike. However, my best sources were The Colorado Trail Foundation (coloradotrail.org) and my brother, who happens to live about ten minutes from the eastern terminus of the trail. Dan had hiked and/or mountain biked a few of the early segments of the trail and had a self-proclaimed good feel for the weather conditions I was likely to face. The Foundation sells three different guidebooks on the trail and I purchased, and studied, all of them.

Timing was a fairly critical issue for me. My son, Matt was scheduled to get home from the Peace Corps the first week of August and would only be around a couple weeks before heading off to law school. So, I either had to finish before August 1st, or start after August 15th. Beginning with a rough estimate of covering 100 miles per week, I would either start by June 23rd or not finish until late September. Of the two options, Dan thought the earlier would be best. He stated that I shouldn't have any issues with snow by then and it should be early enough to miss the "monsoon," when nearly every afternoon involves thunderstorms at higher elevations. (Unfortunately, Dan ended up being wrong on both counts, but that's for later chapters.) The plan became to go early, starting on the Summer Solstice: June 21.

Once my start date was set, I created a rough estimated schedule of the entire hike. Using the Colorado Trail Guidebook, I picked spots where I might camp each night. This exercise gave me an estimate of how long it might take to travel between possible resupply locations.

Resupply was another issue to be worked out. This was pretty straightforward as, unlike the AT, there just aren't that many towns to stop at. However, the most likely resupply options are pretty well spaced. I decided on stops at Frisco, Twin Lakes, Salida, Lake City and Silverton which were each 70-100 trail miles apart.

As I haven't thru-hiked a long trail before, I wanted to keep the resupplies as foolproof as possible. For the most part, this meant mailing packages to myself to be held at the local post offices. Each package would contain all the food I would need for the next stretch, as well as consumables such as travel sized toothpaste, contact lens solution, sunscreen, laundry detergent and the like. The food was split into daily rations, which I hoped would be enough.

Since I could never figure out how I could visit the Laundromat and wash all my clothes at once without being arrested for public indecency, I also included some "throw away" clothes to wear. Yep, each box contained an old, stained, threadbare t-shirt and a ratty pair of pants or shorts. Other than perhaps irritating the fashion police, I'd be able to clean all my trail clothes in one load without running afoul of the law.

The boxes would be sent to Twin Lakes, Salida and Lake City. My brother Dan would meet me for some hiking at Frisco, so he could bring me that box. By the time I got to Silverton, I figured I'd be so sick of the food I'd been shipping to myself that I'd be better off with a grocery store resupply.

After a couple shake down trips on the AT, I had my equipment list complete. There was only one more item to get checked out.

Chapter 4: Getting Physical

I like to think that, physically, I'm in good enough shape to hike the Colorado Trail. I ran (slowly) two marathons last year, one of them in Colorado's Front Range. I also finished a few triathlons this spring. However, as I was planning on solo backpacking across 8 mountain ranges while my age is on the wrong side of 50, I thought it best to get a checkup first.

After initial pleasantries, the first thing the Doctor said was, "Your neck looks big."

"Thanks Doc," I replied, "I have been working out. I'm thinking my shoulders and chest might be a little bigger too."

Apparently what he meant was that my thyroid looked enlarged. He said I should get an ultrasound right away as enlarged thyroids can turn cancerous on you. He asked if there was any family history of thyroid issues. I replied, "Not really. Other than my mom had her's removed, and my dad's mom actually died from her thyroid. Oh, and my one brother is on thyroid medication. Other than that though, no history at all."

"Get that ultrasound ASAP."

"I'm all over it Doc." (As soon as I get back from the hike.)

Later in the physical the Doctor asked about my drinking habits. I responded truthfully; that I rarely drink a lot, but do have a beer or two nearly every day. Satisfied with that answer, he switched subjects to my prostate health as he pulled a glove on. “How often do you get up during the night to go to the bathroom?”

I replied, “Once or twice. However, the last time I didn’t have a drink before bed, I slept straight through till morning, no problem.”

“Well, if you sleep through the night, no need to check; your prostate is fine,” he stated as he peeled the glove back off with a sigh of relief that nearly matched mine. I didn’t have the heart to tell him that the last time I didn’t have a drink before bed, it was 1997.

So the bottom line is; looks like my health is assured. It’s time to hike.

Chapter 5: Limping onto the Trail

A major benefit in choosing to hike the Colorado Trail is that my brother Dan lives less than ten minutes from its eastern end, south of Denver. He was happy to provide support and was eager to even hike a bit of it with me. Easing into the hike became part of the plan. The Colorado Trail is divided into 28 "segments" with access at the end of each segment. With some segments, unless you have a Jeep, the access is theoretical, but it is there nevertheless. We would "day hike" the first two sections before I had to strap on the big pack and be self-sufficient.

With the day to start hiking the Colorado Trail fast approaching, I was expecting a bit of apprehension, but not absolute dread. However, that started building about two weeks out when my left foot started hurting, especially my toes. A visit to a Podiatrist resulted in a diagnosis of a neuroma, or inflamed/enlarged nerves in the foot. There were several possible treatments, but none included hiking 500 miles on the bad foot. The Doc was sure he could fix me up with some shoe inserts he would create on the spot. In fact, he described himself as the Picasso of Podiatrists. He was an artist; but rather than working in oils or watercolor, he worked in feet. I left with my inserts.

The day before I was to start driving west to Denver, I was back at Picasso's, my foot only minimally better. A cortisone shot to the worst spot seemed promising. With 2 days to rest my foot during the drive out, I was hoping for some relief. I walked as little as possible and skipped gears on the six speed whenever I could in an effort to keep the foot off the clutch. (Yea, it was that bad.) By the time I arrived at my brother's, I was hoping the rest and shot had worked their magic. I would start hiking on June 21, the longest day of the year.

The morning the trip was to start, I swung my feet off the bed, stood up and nearly dropped to the floor in pain. Generally, I tend to put up with pain pretty well. I've been told by medical personnel that I "have a high pain tolerance." I've been told by non-medical former friends that I'm "just insensitive." So, for my foot to bother me this much before I even started wasn't looking good at all. The foot felt a little better with shoes/insert in place so I pulled those on and took twice the recommended dosage of Aleve along with a dose of the wonder drug of the 1960s, Anacin.

Dan was to drop me at Waterton Canyon, the start of the trail, at 6 AM, drive to parking 17 miles down the trail then start hiking my way till we met. Watching me limp from the car, he became concerned (an emotion he rarely shows when it involves others) and decided to hike with me for a while.

The trail itself began with 6 easy miles along the South Platte River, but the canyon scenery was gorgeous. As we walked the first couple miles, the foot improved to tolerable. Confident I was good for the day, Dan returned to his car and I began to relax and enjoy the beauty.

It wasn't long before the first wildlife sighting as a herd of bighorn sheep makes the canyon its home. With the sun shining and temps in the 60s, my day was improving dramatically.

Once at the end of the canyon, about 6 1/2 miles in, the trail started climbing gradually through a pine forest into what is known as the Rampart Range. For several miles, switchbacks kept increasing the elevation to a peak of 7,500 feet at about mile 13. Through the higher areas there are views of the taller mountains that loomed in my future.

The foot was holding up, but about this time I began to wonder, "Where the hell is my brother?" (Cell service on the trail is spotty at best.) A mountain biker was stopped along the trail and I asked if he'd noticed anyone walking my way. "What does he look like?"

I replied, "like me but uglier." The biker stated, "Yea, I talked to him, he described you the exact same way." Sure enough we met up shortly thereafter and hiked together down the long decline to the parking lot. We got glimpses of what the next day's hike would hold in store for me, a long climb into the area decimated by 1996 Buffalo Creek Fire. After nearly eight hours of hiking though, it was time to ice my foot and get a good meal.

Day 2 began with Dan dropping me off at the South Platte River Trailhead, the beginning of Segment 2. At that point, the trail was at an elevation of 6,100 feet. It quickly began climbing out of the river valley lush with pine trees into a huge area still scarred from a fire that burned 18 years earlier. Along the way, the trail rose to about 7,800 feet, significantly surpassing the highest point on the Appalachian Trail (6,625 feet). The trail stays above that mark for the duration of its length.

With the trees burned off, the experience was quite a bit different, but not bad. Wildflowers were abundant. As the miles passed the wildlife began to show itself as well. Far from being desolate, the area contained numerous butterflies, chipmunks, rabbits and deer.

Stopping for a break, the only noise was the breeze on distant mountaintops, at least until some hummingbirds began working nearby flowers and added the propeller like sound of their wing beats. A deep blue sky completed the relaxing scene.

As I neared the end of the day's 11 mile section, I once again met up with my brother. A second breakfast and a nap while I was hiking had him refreshed. As we neared the car, thunderstorms began forming to the west and were heading our way. Luckily we finished in time to wait out the storm at a local brewpub. The previous two days of mountain hiking followed by a couple beers and a comfortable bed turned out to be a pretty good plan. However, all good things must end and the real work of this trip was ready to begin.

Chapter 6: The Weight

In my experience, carrying too much weight while backpacking may be the surest way to have a miserable trip, or even not finish. This is especially true on a long trip like the Colorado Trail. So, I've worked hard, and spent significant sums, trying to keep my pack as light as possible to insure that the load feels *right on me.*

Actually, spending money on lighter gear is the easy, and fun, part of getting a lighter pack weight. Dropping a couple hundred on a new pack saved me over two pounds before I even started filling it. Spending more money on a new tent and sleeping bag knocked off another three pounds or so. As a bonus, the new stuff packs up smaller, which helps to make up for the fact that my new lighter pack can't hold as much as my old version.

About the time I bought a titanium spork, I realized I had reached the end of buying my way to a lighter load. Any more savings was only going to come from increasingly tougher decisions.

Sure, it gets cold at night in the mountains, but did I really need a fleece and a long sleeve shirt? Shivering doesn't weigh anything; leave the shirt. On the other hand, sawing the handle off the toothbrush seemed a tad extreme for the weight savings. Skimping on toilet paper to save an ounce appeared to be a fool's choice as well.

On shorter trips, the pack typically contains a flask (or possibly two). For this trip I made the (heart wrenching) decision to travel alcohol free, saving over two pounds. A much smarter approach would be to binge drink when I reach towns. (Note to self: rewrite the previous sentence before publishing. Don't believe the wording shows me in the best light.)

Of course, with the hike being entirely within the state of Colorado, there was a lighter, legal option for a Rocky Mountain High while out on the trail. However, I planned to steer clear of the weed shops for a number of reasons, not the least of which is weight related. I've spent quite a bit of time and effort picking meals and weighing out snacks so I had just enough to get by. I expected to be hungry fairly often as it was. A good case of the munchies could prove disastrous for my rationing plan.

However, I warned those reading my blog that, "if my writing becomes unintelligible at some point, or worse a final post says something like, 'Dude, check out this shot of me holding a bear cub I just found,' you'll know I've fallen prey to reefer madness."

Anyway, the pack and gear tipped the scales at 21 pounds. Add four days of food and two liters of water and I would be hauling 31 pounds on my back, hopefully not too bad.

Chapter 7: Reality begins

Day 3 began with a longer drive as I was getting further from Denver with each hike. The day was also different as instead of a five pound daypack, I was carrying everything needed to get to Frisco, Colorado, five days and 76 miles distant.

Driving out to the Little Scraggy Trailhead, we passed a bull elk waiting to cross the highway. The animals may have been out, but people were not. Arriving at the trailhead at 6:30, we were the only car. The sky was absolutely clear, but it was only 42 degrees. Maybe I should have packed that long sleeve shirt.

The trail was void of other hikers as well, but again the scenery did not disappoint. Climbing to still higher elevations, I walked through alpine meadows filled with wildflowers and huge stands of aspen trees. Walking quietly, I startled multiple deer.

Throughout the crystal clear morning, I got numerous views of the still bigger mountains awaiting me to the west. Several still had quite a bit of snow on them. Maybe I really should have packed that long sleeve shirt.

The weather was a repeat of the day before, with thunderstorms building up in the afternoon. There was no brewpub to escape to anymore though. Luckily, I was able to hike into the Lost Creek Wilderness Area as I had planned, set up camp and eat dinner before the lightning and rain started pounding. The temperature dropped fast and lightning was hitting all around as I lay in the tent. I normally use my fleece for a pillow, but instead needed to wear it. An interesting evening to say the least. On the plus side, my foot was staying "tolerable."

As I did every evening while on the trail, I sent a signal back home using the Spot Satellite Tracker. This is a useful piece of electronics. Without needing cell service, it allows one to send prewritten messages out to friends or family via email or text, along with a Google map of the present location. I had the option of four messages. Mine were variations of, I'm OK, I'm OK and will make it to town tomorrow, I need help, but it's not life threatening (lost or a sprained ankle), and a direct message to Search and Rescue. (A bear is chewing on me or my leg bone is on the wrong side of my skin.) The Spot is well worth the cost and weight (5 ounces), for peace of mind if nothing else.

Day 4 began with cool and clear weather. The trail started climbing in a hurry, gaining over 1,000 feet of elevation in a couple miles. It was like taking the stairs at a fifty story building (Cincinnati readers think Carew Tower), twice, with a backpack, and with 30% less oxygen than normal.

On the climb I ran into two other thru-hikers, Eric and Virginia. They planned to skip the section from Kenosha Pass to Salida to avoid any snow. They'll pick up that section later in the summer. I may wish I had that long sleeve shirt yet.

After the climb, the trail entered a beautiful wide valley with crystal clear Lost Creek running through it. It was perfect timing as I was running low on water. No matter how good the water looks, I do filter it however. After getting the water I followed the trail upstream. A small herd of elk crossed the creek in front of me. I assume the filter can handle elk pee.

The valley continued for several miles and I noticed at least 6 beaver dams on the creek. I was really hoping the filter handled beaver poo as well.

The day was going to be a long one as I planned to go 18 miles. I was tired and limping when I arrived at the area I planned to camp. There were only 2 flat spots around and surprisingly, both were taken. There was nothing to do but keep walking. Hungry as I was, I began eating trail mix while I walked. Not paying attention, I rolled my ankle on a rock, crashed to the ground and to top it off, damaged my camera. Not my best moment. On the bright side, my twisted ankle took my mind off the pain in my foot. As my knee was bleeding, it was time to break out the massive first aid kit. An alcohol wipe and band aid took care of most of the issue. I'd have to be careful going forward. The first aid supplies were nearly half gone.

After limping another mile or so, I spotted a small flat area (there are less of them than you would imagine) and called it a day. Total distance for the day was 20 1/2 miles.

Day 5 started cool and cloudy. After the tough day yesterday I was hoping for more of a "bluebird" day. Ten miles was all I was shooting for. After a short climb, I was at the bottom of another wide valley. The views were great and I was soon in a huge grove of Aspen, packed full of wildflowers and even bluebirds. The sky cleared to a beautiful deep blue. My foot and ankle were both behaving. As I approached Kenosha Pass, the views of the snow covered peaks in the distance just kept getting better and better. The scene was so beautiful, it took my breath away. It was that or the fact I was at over 10,000 feet.

The trail eventually drops out of the Kenosha Mountains to the pass at a Forest Service campground. I got to eat lunch at a real picnic table! There was even an indoor toilet. I didn't really need it, but couldn't pass up the opportunity to lighten my load in comfort.

The guidebook stated there was water available in the area, but I couldn't find any. No way they meant the pond I walked by. Since there were only 3 more miles to cover to reach a campsite next to a stream, I decided to head on with about 6 ounces of water left on me.

After a mile of climbing, I was draining the bottle when a woman walked up with a small pack. In response to her question, I mentioned hiking the Colorado Trail. She was very interested and asked quite a few questions. One question I ask her was if there was any water closer than 2 miles. “Why none I’m aware of,” she stated while she pulled a full liter of bottled water out of her pack, broke the seal and took a big slug.

That was my cue to cut the conversation short and knock out the last 2 miles. Thunderclouds were building fast over the nearby peaks and it started looking like it would be a photo finish with the rain. Luckily, because of cutting the conversation short, there was just enough time to set up camp, filter some water and be ready to nap through the storm. Seventy five miles down, 410 to go.

Chapter 8: Up to the Divide

"I'll fly on a plane and people will look out the window at thirty thousand feet and say, 'Isn't this view good enough for you?' And I say no, it's not good enough. I didn't earn it. In the mountains, I earn it."

Mark Obmascik

DAY 6 started out cold and clear. At 6 am I began hiking. In 3 miles there was a creek which would be my last chance for water for 11 miles which included a 2,000 foot climb into the Front Range Mountains and the Continental Divide. Just breaking camp at the creek were 2 other thru-hikers, Golden and Wildflower.

Golden was in her early twenties and Wildflower her 50s, but both were accomplished backpackers, having thru-hiked the Appalachian Trail in 2012. We leapfrogged each other up the long grind as the snowcapped mountains I had been seeing for days got dramatically closer. About halfway up (11,000 feet) we began seeing small piles of snow.

By the time we broke above tree line, the piles were no longer small. Long ridges of deep snow blocked the trail and required detours. Luckily, the windswept saddle between two peaks, where we were headed, was free of much snow. Once we reached the divide, the view was unbelievable. It was cold, windy and a hell of a hike to get there, but well worth the price of admission. Little did we know at that point though, that the price for the view was going to be significantly higher than we had already paid.

After several pictures, including celebratory selfies, it was time to start down the west side of the divide. It quickly became evident that getting back down would not be a walk in the park (even though that's what it was). The trail at that point dropped very little and was cut into the steep mountainside. As we continued, the snow ridges reappeared, then became deeper and more numerous. Each ridge had to be hiked around, over or through, none of which were good options. Several times I was on top of a 4 to 6 foot tall ridge when the crusty surface would give way and put me instantly ass deep in snow, otherwise known as post holing. Some of the ridges ended with a wall of snow that just had to be ridden down. It was hard enough work that I stayed warm just wearing shorts and a t-shirt.

After a mile or so, we were exhausted and stopped for lunch. Wildflower sat against a tree and I noticed a good size gash in her leg. As she mopped up the blood she talked about how her "country club" friends didn't understand why she liked backpacking so much. "That's true," I remarked, "Some people just don't appreciate how much fun it is to be laying in the snow….on the side of a mountain… bleeding."

Eventually, the snow ridges got smaller and further apart and hiking became normal again. We exchanged small talk and at one point Golden asked what music I would use if I was creating a sound track for the trail. I mentioned Bob Seger (Roll Me Away), Stephen Stills (Colorado) and of course a big helping of John Denver. That was one of those moments when you realize how far apart experiences are across generations. "Who's John Denver?"

I had actually downloaded several John Denver songs for this very trip, and Golden got to hear Rocky Mountain High and a few others for the first time while actually high up in the Rockies. She said she really liked him, but may have just been being polite. Hard to tell. We definitely agreed that the views mean much more when you have to earn them like we had.

Eventually we got low enough to reach running water and replenish our supplies. Golden and Wildflower were on a mission to put in more miles to make it into the town of Breckenridge early the next day. I was beat from the day's workout, pulled into the first good looking camp spot and bid them farewell. Apparently though, I set my tent up too close to a squirrel's abode for his liking. As I lay in my sleeping bag writing, he stood just outside the tent chattering at me. It would be a long evening.

Chapter 9: Frisco

Day 7 dawned clear and cool. I had 13 miles to reach the end of Section 6 where's there's a bus stop and a ride to the towns of Breckenridge and Frisco. I had a hotel room reserved in Frisco, but still had some walking to do first. Almost immediately there were more jaw dropping views. A mountain biker rode up and asked if I were a thru-hiker. A yes answer brought a pronouncement that the next section of the trail had 20 feet of snow on it. He then began to quiz me about local history and politics. Despite answering every question with, "I wouldn't know. I'm from Cincinnati," the interrogation continued. Eventually I changed my answer to, "have a good ride," and moved on.

Over the next few miles I met a few other hikers coming the other way. All asked if I were a thru-hiker. Apparently it was becoming obvious. I wondered, was it the confident walk? The filling out of the neck beard? The smell? Hmmm.

There were still 8 miles to go when I spotted Frisco down in a pretty valley, but it was enough to pick up the pace. My main obstacle, besides the distance, was walking through areas where the pine bark beetle infestation was being treated. By treated, I mean every tree for acres was cut down and chipped up. When walking these stretches, plan on needing sunscreen.

Luck was on my side as a bus and I arrived at the stop at the exact same time. Not ten minutes later I was checking into the Snowshoe Inn on Main Street in Frisco. It's the perfect location, right at a bus stop and within 100 yards of a

Laundromat, the Backcountry Brewery and the Silverheels Bar and Grill (spring for the crab stuffed trout). A glance in the mirror was a bit surprising. While I hadn't been overly hungry on the trail, it was obvious that I'd already lost ten pounds or so. I needed to cram in the calories while in town.

My brother Dan drove down and we planned to take advantage of the great bus service to day hike or "slack pack" (walk without my tent, sleeping bag, etc.) the next section.

Day 8 dawned cloudy and cold. "The worst hike ever." Dan and I planned to get started early on my slack pack of Segment 7. We grabbed a quick breakfast at the only place open in Frisco at 6 am, (Starbucks) and drove up to Copper Ski Resort, where the section ended. Because this 14 mile section crested the Tenmile Mountain Range close to its finish, we decided to hike it backwards. This gave us the benefit of tackling the tough, uphill climb first, while we were fresh, and also get us out of the higher elevations earlier, in case of afternoon thunderstorms.

The hike started at nearly 10,000 feet and immediately began an unrelenting climb from there. We were heading for 12,500 feet, the highest of the trip so far and the trail appeared to be in a hurry to get us there. As we climbed in altitude, the breeze picked up as well. The occasional glimpse of the mountaintops looked intimidating. After about 3 miles, we broke past tree line and lost our protection against the ever strengthening wind. On nearly every day of the trip to this point, early morning clouds would quickly dissipate, but not this day. No sun to warm us up.

For the last two miles before the high point, the area is considered to be tundra. Nothing of any size can grow in the harsh environment so there in no protection from the elements. I was getting hungry and thirsty, but there was no way it was worth stopping. The temperature was down around freezing and the wind had to be at least 50 mph. We looked like a scene from the Weather Channel's Storm Report. The only positive to the situation was there was little snow to deal with. It had all been blown off the mountain.

Eventually we were able to reach the high point and just enough beyond to get a little protection from the wind. Though we had enough warm clothing, neither of us had brought gloves (it was nearly July) and our hands were suffering. Dan's shoe became untied, and he was unable to take care of it. My hands were a little better and so I was able to tie it for him. It did take several tries to get my zipper back up after taking a leak, however. Thankfully Dan didn't have to go, because there would be no help forthcoming.

The other interesting news was that I figured out where all the snow went that had been blown off the other side of the mountain. We were going to have to descend through a winter wonderland.

The trail began dropping by being cut at an angle into the steep mountainside. Large areas were covered by snowfields that alternated between icy (think bobsled run) and soft enough to drop into it crotch deep. Needless to say, progress was slow. In spots where the trail was covered, we also had to guess where it actually was, and look to pick it up at the next clear area. Dan and I did a bit of reminiscing through here. "Remember how we would want to go fishing or canoeing on the very first day of spring? Dad would say, 'You guys are always rushing the season.' You think he might have had a point?"

"Nah."

Eventually we made it to tree line, where things should get better, but not here. The snow covered everything, so there was no way to know where the trail was. The many meltwater creeks were running underneath the snow, so there was the added possibility of dropping through the snow into some mighty chilly water.

There were some footprints in this softer snow, so we followed those for a while; until they stopped. I have to say, that was a bad feeling. Miles from the finish. No one else around. No trail. No indication of a trail. The final fall back was my GPS, on which I had downloaded some waypoints of the trail. The next waypoint was a half mile away, so we just plowed in that general direction until we were close to it. The next waypoint was another half mile away so we repeated the process. By then there were some bare spots on the ground and we picked up the trail again. Once Dan got all the ice out his shoes, we were merrily strolling down the trail, only 6 miles to go. The sun even came out!

Just so things wouldn't be too easy, with about two miles to go, we hit another area where all the trees had been cut to fight the pine bark beetle. The work had decimated the trail and once again we were cross country orienteering with the GPS.

Once we made the bus stop it was straight to the Backcountry Brewery. Time for an easy decision: take a day off!

Chapter 10: Snow in July

"There is wisdom in climbing mountains... For they teach us how truly small we are."
Jeff Wheeler

Day 10 started clear and cool, staying sunny all day. The next section of trail also climbed to well over 12,000 feet, so it was going to be another day with snow. The Colorado Trail website had listed the previous two segments as passable. Today's section was listed as heavy snow; not a word about passable. Back on my own, I climbed out of the Copper Mountain ski resort, spotting snow at an elevation of 10,400; not a good sign. However, some ptarmigans and deer gave me something else to think about.

Soon there was a repeat of the last two hikes with ridges of snow that had to be climbed over or plowed through. It was looking like a long day until I hit tree line, where there was a surprising absence of heavy accumulation. The occasional snow field was crusted over enough, that, at least for the moment, I could walk over rather than post hole. A couple snowfields did get the heart rate up in that large creeks disappeared into them. I knew if the snow gave way and dropped me into the creek, it would not be pretty.

By the time I reached the first pass at nearly 12,000 feet, I was ready for an early lunch. Sitting on some rubble enjoying yet another jaw dropping landscape I had the feeling I was not alone. One by one, marmots began popping out of the rocks all around me. Startle one and you'll know why they have the endearing nickname of "whistle pig."

Afternoon brought more snowfields to cross. It is amazing to me how quickly the tundra wildflowers follow the melting snow. There were often blooming flowers when there had to be snow just a day or two before. After over three miles in heavy snow above 12,000 feet, the trail finally headed down to a more reasonable 10,000 where I set up my tent alongside a rushing stream known as Cataract Creek.

A couple hours later, who shows up but Golden and Wildflower. They had started their day about 2 miles behind me but hiked the extra distance to catch up. They are some serious hikers.

For dinner, Golden told me she had a bag of scrambled eggs from the hostel they stayed in two nights ago and offered me some. “They’re green!” I replied when I spotted her offering. “That’s the avocado,” she stated. “It has some vegetarian ham in it too.”

Despite still being hungry after my freeze dried entrée; from somewhere deep in the recesses of my mind I remembered that I should not and could not eat green eggs and ham. I declined the offer.

Day 11 was clear all day. I thought I heard a bear in camp during the night, but apparently it was Golden finding out that green eggs and ham weren’t a good idea for her either. She and Wildflower were planning on hitching a ride into Leadville for food of a different color. I’d planned on a 20 mile day and so packed up and headed out early.

Much of the trail through this area is on old Forest Service roads, so it’s a tad boring, but the miles were easy. Along the way, an older couple walked towards me and asked about some side trails. I was not much help, but showed them my maps. After a short “domestic” they turned around and started hiking with me, back the way they came. They were pretty interesting to talk to and were the stereotypical couple that had been together so long they began to resemble each other. They talked alike, dressed somewhat the same and even had matching sideburns.

The easy miles ended abruptly when I got to the Holy Cross Wilderness Area. In a mile I climbed close to 1,000 feet and was back over 11,000. (It felt more like the "Holy Crap" Wilderness Area.) I had hoped because I remained a bit lower than yesterday, that there'd be no snow to contend with. Man was I ever wrong. It was back to plowing through drifts and post holing. Despite having waterproof shoes, there was no way to avoid wet feet for 3 of the last 4 days, and it was starting to take a toll. No one has ever said to me, "Your feet look pretty," but they've rarely looked as nasty as they did then. I stopped a couple times to attempt to dry my socks in the sun, but eventually the only thing that improved the situation was taping over the blisters with duct tape. That actually helped quite a bit. After 20 miles for the day though, I was pretty much worn out. I set up camp near a small pond, but still at an elevation of 11,000 feet. The sky was still clear. The campsite was partially covered in snow. A chilly night was in the cards. On the plus side, mosquitos, which had become surprisingly troublesome, were rendered too cold to fly.

Chapter 11: Getting a Little Company

Day 12 started like nearly every day, cool and sunny. Despite temperatures that put a bit of frost on the tent, I had slept well.

Soon after leaving the Holy Cross Wilderness, I entered the Mt Massive Wilderness area. Much of the day was spent in heavy pine forest, with just an occasional glimpse of the rightly named Mt Massive. At 14,421 feet tall, it's a few feet shorter than nearby Mt Elbert, tallest in the state, but appears to be a bigger rock.

My brother Bob had flown out to visit and he and Dan walked towards me from the other end of the segment. With 4 miles left in a 16 mile day, we met up. It was great to see them. Even better, Bob shouldered my pack the rest of the way to the car.

First we drove to the Twin Lakes General Store to pick up a box I'd mailed to myself. Other than looking like it had been kicked from Cincinnati to Colorado, it was fine. The box contained all my food for the next section along with a few travel sized "consumables" such as sunblock, toothpaste and contact lens solution.

After checking in at the Leadville Super 8, (*The only thing we overlook is the slag heap,*) it's off to the Golden Burro bar and grill. We all got bean burritos, very tasty and filling. However, they should not be served to anyone over 65; at least not if you share a motel room with them.

Day 13 was yet another sunny day, but getting warmer. The effort was almost like taking a day off. We hiked a short (12 mile) section that's relatively flat and the best part was my brother Bob carried a daypack with everything we might need for the day. I carried absolutely nothing and felt like I was floating. Dan walked with us for the first mile or so, then headed back to the car so he could meet us near the end of the day's hike (after a nap).

With no pack and easy conversation, the miles flew by. The scenery alternated between conifers and huge groves of aspen, with occasional glimpses of Mt Elbert and Massive. After about six miles we started seeing Twin Lakes. Despite its name, there's really only one lake that just gets narrow in the middle. Regardless, it was a pretty sight as we dropped out of the woods to walk along the bank. You'd think that would be an interesting section, but it was 4 miles long with absolutely no shade. By then, it was around noon and the sun began to roast me through the sunscreen.

With about two miles of lakeshore to go, Dan came walking up with a hiker he had met. Marvin was another thru-hiker that skipped the snow area and was hiking back toward it. Dan took great pleasure in letting him know he'd still be dealing with snow (though much less than even a few days ago).

The afternoon job for me was the Laundromat, though I can't say the washing got my socks to smell fresh. Much better, but not fresh. While I was out, I also picked up some "liquid skin" to paint over, and hopefully protect my blisters. Dan and Bob filled the time catching up on their beauty sleep.

That evening, it was back to the Golden Burro, though no one was allowed the get burritos. After buffalo burgers all around, there was still time to find a TV and watch the Rockies lose another ball game. All in all, a great change of pace. I'm 180 miles deep into the hike.

Chapter 12: Wishing

The morning of day 14, sunny and warm of course, I was back to hiking on my own. Dan and Bob drove me back to where we had stopped the day before, helped me on with my pack and left me with words of encouragement. Even though I've always known it, it's nice to be reminded how much they care.

Walking along Twin Lakes first thing in the morning I got some tremendous views of the mountains reflected in the water. Soon however, it was time to start climbing, which was getting less fun each time.

Part of the route was along Forest Service Roads and through their camping areas, which are pretty basic. Due to the Independence Day holiday, they were fairly crowded though.

As I was walking through, a guy ran up and asked if I were a thru-hiker. When I said yes, he told me I was off the trail. He stated I probably missed the turn about 100 feet back because, "those assholes are camped right on the trail."

I walked back with the guy and sure enough, there was the trail, right between an "asshole's" big wall tent and some bike trailers. As I thanked him and turned to leave, his wife/girlfriend came up offering me a banana, some juice and to take my trash. Now that's pretty friendly.

After walking a few more miles of Forest Service roads, I began to drop into the Clear Creek Valley. In stark contrast to the forests I'd been walking through, this hillside, with a full southern exposure, only supported scrub growth and even some small cacti. Of course, to be consistent with everywhere else I'd been on the trail, the cacti were in bloom.

As I ate lunch by the creek, a day hiker walked by and asked about my hike. After a few minutes he offered me some water. Not sure he believed me when I pointed at the creek and said I had plenty.

After lunch I started on the first of several major climbs to be "conquered." Climbing close to 3,000 feet over 4 miles slowed progress to a crawl. Worse yet, short rain showers were hitting about every half hour, forcing me to put on and take off rainwear several times.

As I finally arrived where I had planned to camp for the night, it began to sprinkle. Rather than rush to put up the tent, I thought I'd wait out another "short" shower, then set up. A half hour later, I was still standing under a pine tree watching the pouring rain turn my chosen spot into a quagmire. After an hour and a half, a short break in the rain lasted just long enough to throw up the tent and pile everything, including myself, inside to wait out the next downpour. The weather finally cleared at dark. It made for a late dinner. You'd think freeze dried sweet and sour pork would be worth the wait, but it's not.

I'm sure some people think that backpacking for 500 miles is pure, unadulterated fun. Those people would be wrong. Actually, for the most part they are right. There are times though when they are very wrong. Besides the sheer effort of hauling yourself, and everything thing you need to be comfortable (or at least survive) through high altitude mountainous wilderness, you also have the weight of any doubts, fears and unhappiness that you drag along. Not always being a "glass half full" guy results in the figurative weight I carry getting fairly significant at times. However, it hasn't been tough to handle when the sun is shining and the views are great. When they're not though, conditions can get you wishing that the hike was over.

Sore tired legs, tasteless meals that don't satisfy and having to crap in a hole you just dug are difficulties that you accept in exchange for beautiful surroundings and a tremendous feeling of accomplishment. Generally a pretty good trade, but not always. Hours of rain can wash out whatever positive emotion you woke up with. You wish the sun would come out, but it doesn't. You wish for a worthwhile view, but rain and fog restricts your sight and dampens your spirit, clothes and equipment. When the rain eases up, the mosquitos come out. With nothing positive to occupy your mind, it starts to wander to things you shouldn't dwell on; the knee that is starting to hurt, the taste of this morning's freeze dried eggs. You relive old relationships, wishing you could change things you did wrong.

Eventually, you leave the past and just start wishing for a better here and now. By the end of the day things get pretty simple. You wish only for dry clothes, a cold beer and a warm place to take a dump. However, what you have is a wet tent and you're 3 days away from the closest hotel. As you lay in your smelly, damp sleeping bag, you wish the hike was over, but it's not.

At times like these, rather than quit, you need to fight the negativity. For some, a positive childhood memory will do the trick. I think of my dear old Mom's favorite saying. She used it often when, as a young boy, I would tell her about what I wanted for dinner or just something I wished for. I can almost hear her now. "Wish in one hand and crap in the other; see which one fills up first."

With warm memories of childhood floating through my head, I drift off to sleep. 300 miles to go.

Chapter 13: Prediction? Pain

Reporter: *Clubber, what's your prediction for the fight?*
Clubber Lang (as poignantly played by Mr. T in Rocky 3): *Prediction? Pain.*

Now there's no way to write about being in the Rockies without, at some point, tying it into the Rocky movie franchise.

Now there have been times in the past when running, triathlons or other sports where I felt I could beat another opponent. I've even felt I could "beat" a course I was familiar with. Five hundred miles of the Rocky Mountains is a different story. If you try to beat the mountains, as Clubber said, you just get pain. Or, as Adrian screeched at Rocky as he was headed to Moscow to fight the big Russian, "You can't win!" (By the way, thanks for the support there, Adrian.)

The Rocky Mountains cannot be beaten. They are too tall, too vast and have the staying power of….hell, a mountain.

For the first two weeks of this trip, I was "winning." I had created a schedule to follow and was not only meeting it, despite various foot/ankle injuries, I was beating it.

Day 15 brought me back to reality. I was hiking into the Collegiate Mountains. After packing up a wet camp from the previous night's rain, I was looking at two huge climbs. Straight from camp there is a 1,400 foot climb that took me near 12,000 feet onto Mt Harvard. (That's quite a bit higher than Mt Saint Joe or Mt Adams in Cincinnati.) Between the lousy camp the night before, the climb and the intense sun above tree line, I was already feeling worn out and it was only 9 am.

After a short drop, it was back up Mt Columbia and maybe a couple community college peaks as well. A long downgrade had me having a late lunch down around 9,000 feet. There were some nice camping spots there, but my schedule had me getting past Mt Yale yet that day. The climb was the steepest I'd yet encountered and I was suffering with every step. Yale's entrance exam was more than I could handle and the mountain may have discovered my "Achilles Heel." Ironically enough, that was my Achilles tendon, which was hurting worse with each step.

As I struggled up the cliff disguised as a trail, I met a woman and her dog heading down. She asked if I was a thru-hiker (had to be the neck beard) and we talked about the trail. When I mentioned how steep the trail was at that point, she cheerfully replied, "Oh, it gets steeper!"

Unbelievably, it turned out that she was right. As I walked, it was like I was face to face with the trail. At this point I finally decided that I needed to stop trying to meet an arbitrary schedule and just take what the mountains would give. Thankfully what the mountain gave me was a beautiful alpine meadow about halfway up Yale. A stream was nearby, but far enough away to not draw mosquitoes. A small grove of pine protected a flat area just right for the tent, but left in enough breeze to dry yesterday's rain off the material. I had plenty of time to take a nap and enjoy the evening. The weather was gorgeous and I was able to relax and recharge. The world was a much better place than it had been just a few hours earlier.

Also on the site was an old abandoned cabin. It seemed rather symbolic of the mountain's infinite patience. The cabin was about halfway back to being reabsorbed by the mountain and Mt Yale had all the time in the world to finish the project.

Chapter 14: Closing in on Halfway

Day 16 started off, you guessed it, sunny and cool. After a short, but hard grind to the high point on Yale, there is a sharp downhill, then rolling for over 20 miles. It looked like a day to get in some decent mileage. Starting out, my Achilles tendon even felt fine. Hopefully, that was a one-time occurrence. The sky stayed mostly clear throughout the morning and I was coating myself with sunscreen by 8 am. Not only was much of the trail that day in the open, what woods it traveled through were relatively thin. Considering that the sun's intensity at 10,000 feet is 50% stronger than at sea level. It doesn't take long to figure out that sunscreen is a real necessity on the trail.

After settling in to a shady spot for lunch, I apparently was once again irritating a squirrel. As he chattered at me, I pulled out the camera to get a shot of him. He in turn continued to get closer. It seemed cute until he kept closing in and started baring those tiny little buck teeth. At the same time, it appeared his nest mate was executing a flanking maneuver to block my escape. I decided that I had enough squirrel pictures and it was time to move on.

There must be some problems getting a trail corridor near the town of Mt Princeton. The trail dumped onto a Forest Service road, then through a private "dude ranch" and finally onto paved roads for nearly 6 miles. If anyone decides to skip that portion, they have my blessing. The only saving grace of that desolate stretch was walking right by (and into) the Mt Princeton Hot Springs Country Store. I took a short snack break that included a Hot Pocket made my usual way (still frozen on one end and nuclear hot at the other), cheese, yogurt, a quart of ice cream and some pop. Hopefully that would tide me over till dinner. My appetite had really kicked in over the last few days and I was constantly hungry. Finally back on trail at the far side of town, there is a sharp climb and I end the day overlooking the town with a great view of the chalky white cliffs of Mt Princeton and the surrounding hills. I was finally through the Collegiate Peaks!

Surprisingly enough, day 17 started off clear and warm. As I left town the night before, I grabbed 2 1/2 liters of water from Chalk Creek that was to last through dinner, breakfast and 6 1/2 miles of trail. Between the dry air, intense sun and hilly terrain, I may have underestimated my liquid requirements. I read somewhere that, when drinking enough, healthy urine is clear. Mine reminded me of orange juice; at least it was pulp free. Orange juice is healthy, isn't it? Regardless, I spent quite a bit of time filtering and drinking water at the first creek I reached.

The stretch alternated between open land and young forest. The trail itself was relatively level. Relatively is the operative term here; this is the Rocky Mountains. During the 19 miles walked this day, I climbed and dropped over 7,000 feet in elevation. Through the day I was close to deer, rabbits, turkeys (with young), and what I think were quail. No more vicious squirrels though. What did get a bit vicious was the weather. By early afternoon thunderstorms were building over the nearby mountaintops. Quickly they spread, any blue sky disappeared, and the rain began. It looked ugly and by the time I put on a rain jacket, pants and a pack cover, (yes, the pack has its own rain jacket) the rain began in earnest. The rumble of thunder was almost constant when the hail started. Luckily the hail stayed somewhat small. Big enough to tell when it hit, but not big enough to hurt. With nothing better to do, I kept walking. Apparently that type of weather has no impact on elk, as a female just stood there and stared as I walked by.

After an hour or so the rain let up and I was closing in on my goal for the day, where the trail crosses Rt. 50. (The very same Rt. 50 that's in Cincinnati.) It was there that I had a cab pick me up and take me to nearby Salida for another day off. I'm now 252 miles deep into the trail; officially over halfway!

Chapter 15: A Family is Born

Since many thru-hikers use hostels to save a few bucks, I thought I'd try a night at the Simple Hostel in Salida while I took a day off. As I was a Hostel Virgin (sounds like a band I could have been in when I was 16), I thought I'd ease into it by getting a private room. It's definitely a different experience. A guy in the living room was playing the guitar, poorly; so I headed onto the porch and talk with a few hikers already there. I'm the only guy with a beer in his hand. I'm also the only guy without a joint in his hand. Eventually I met a hiker called White Pine who was thru-hiking the CT and was a day ahead of me.

The hostel was an interesting experience but I moved out to Super 8 after getting a supply box I had mailed to myself at the Post Office. Also, I was meeting Dan the next morning to slack pack another section. I received a text from Golden and Wildflower saying they were in Salida, wondering where I was. I shared the plan to slack pack and they were all for doing it.

It was clear for the start of day 19 as we walked Segment 15 backward, saving walking up a 9 mile hill. About halfway, we passed White Pine, who was heading the other, more difficult way. We stopped at Monarch Crest for lunch which may have been most beautiful spot so far. After watching the clouds build, we started down in a hurry but not fast enough. Rain and hail started when we were about halfway down from the crest. By the time we got back to Salida however, it was clear again. Dropping the ladies back at the Hostel, Dan and I tried Moonlight Pizza, Wall Bangers and eventually Amicas, which has some great lasagna (I get hungry). It was there we met up with Golden and Wildflower for dinner.

On day 20 (who'd have guessed, clear weather) Dan dropped off Golden, Wildflower and me at the trailhead. We were looking at a 20 mile day to get to Baldy Lake to camp.

One issue for women hikers is guys that try to attach themselves to them or their group through the hike in the hopes romance might bloom in the woods. The situation is common enough on the Appalachian Trail that it has a name, Pink Blazing. Not wanting to be seen as a Pink Blazer, I told them to feel free to move on without me. (There's no doubt they could both out-hike me if they wanted,) They wouldn't hear of it. In fact, Golden began calling us a family.

There was also some discussion of trail names. Most, but not all hikers have a trail name. About half name themselves and the others are named. Somewhere I had read about a woman on the AT that did not yet have a trail name. In the middle of the night she was awakened by stomach cramps, but rather than going out into the dark to relieve herself, had decided to stay in her tent and make use of a Ziploc bag. Things did not go well and in the morning she had a new, rather unflattering trail name. I decided to name myself rather than leave my trail title to fate. ("After the bear attack we just started calling him Lefty.")

The problem is, I already have about 20 names. Ask anybody named James. Besides Jim there's Jimmy, Jim Bob, Jimbo, Jiminy, and so on. It's hard to keep up with. I needed something I could remember. I did however, have one non-James related nickname when I was little. My brother Bob named me after Tarzan's pet lion in the old movies, Simba. Even though I hadn't used it in decades and Disney added a little too much cuteness to it, it beat getting named Snot Ball or Hemorrhoid. Simba it is.

By the time we (mainly me) struggled the full 20 miles to Baldy Lake to camp, there was somebody else already there, none other than White Pine. He had a fire going and we all gathered around it that evening. By morning, the Family Meeting on the day's hiking plan had four in attendance. The Family now had representatives from Georgia, Mississippi, Iowa and Ohio, all the big mountain states.

Chapter 16: Cow Country

Day 21 was a long day. After starting out clear, there was walking through multiple bouts of rain. Golden found a can of peaches along road and, forgetting the green egg fiasco, ate them. We'll see how that goes… Later that day she saw that someone had dumped some trail mix into the road's cattle guard ditch and spent several minutes working on a plan to fish it out before being convinced to move on. I believe she needed to consider packing more food.

That's right though, we were getting into cattle country, mostly rolling land that had been leased out for grazing. The travel was a bit easier and we covered 22 miles that day; with total mileage passing 300.

Day 22 was clear in the morning. As mentioned, we got into cow country the day before, with much more of it today. Rolling hills, going through gates on a regular basis, plenty of cow pies all over. I wasn't in a big rush to drink water from a creek surrounded by cow crap, but was starting to run low. Then a huge bit of trail "magic." At around three miles into the day's hike through a long stretch with no shade was a silver dome tent and a horse trailer. They were set up by a trail angel called Apple. The horse trailer was set up for sheltered sleeping and the dome had coolers full of ice cold pop, Gatorade and water. Coffee and a gas stove to heat water were there too. Quite the treat. I dumped out the filtered cow poop water I already had and filled up with clean stuff.

Just after lunch we were at the start of a 2 1/2 mile long open valley when the afternoon thunderstorm decided to unload on us. There was some fear about lightening but I stated there was no way the lightning would bypass the mountaintops and strike us. I actually told Golden, a former lifeguard, that she was more likely to fall in the nearby creek and drown than be hit by lightning. Amazing how when you say something with confidence, people will believe it. It was a tough stretch for Golden as she is not only afraid of being killed by lightning, but also has an unnatural fear of being trampled by cows; and we had to split a herd to get up the valley. At one point, we even had to walk around a dead cow. Luckily, it didn't appear to have been hit by lightning, or I'd have lost all credibility.

At the end of the valley, the bridge over the Cochetopa Creek was out and I got to use my sandals I've carried for 300 miles. Creek crossings are just one example of how well the trail is designed and maintained. After crossing literally dozens of creeks and streams of all sizes, mostly swelled by snowmelt, this was the first crossing that I had to get my feet wet.

We ended up walking 20 miles and cows and cow pies were with us nearly the whole way. They were even in the La Garita Wilderness area, which was a sad surprise. (That section should be the La Giardia Wilderness.) However considering the steepness of the trail, I have a new respect for a cow's balance and hiking ability. Climbing into the La Garita Mountains we eventually got clear of the cow area and camped in a beautiful spot about 26 miles from Lake City. I was able to make my water last till then. Once again, I only had to worry about drinking elk and beaver poop.

The Family was set to break up, however. White Pine was shooting to climb a 14,000 foot mountain in the morning (San Luis Peak), then head into Creede for a resupply. Golden and Wildflower were ready to walk some huge miles in an effort the get to Lake City for their own resupply as they were nearly out of food. There just weren't enough canned goods lying along the road to fulfill their needs. Just before the big breakup though, we received our second trail magic in one day.

As we walked by one of the trail's access points, we met a woman who was cutting her thru-hike attempt short. Her family was picking her up and we stopped to chat. Suddenly they began pulling out her unused trail food and insisting we take it. There was enough for everyone to make it to Lake City without huge miles or swinging into Creede. Happily, the Family would stay together a while longer. Yet another 20 mile day.

My hike's 23rd day started clear and cold. We began at around 6 AM with a long walk up a beautiful valley. The early start was due to much of the day being above tree line and the recent daily thunderstorms. The three previous big mileage days had taken their toll on me and I was dragging a bit from the get go. The morning consisted of just one hill, but one that was 7 miles long and topped out near 13,000 feet. Before the day was over we dropped and climbed three more times. The hills were killing me and I felt I may be holding the others back. It got me wondering about The Family staying together. I enjoyed the company immensely but considered that I may need to hike at a slower pace. I was keeping an open mind, but thinking I might be better off setting off on my own after Lake City.

As I struggled up to the Continental Divide, I mention that when people over 55 die walking to the fridge, it's no longer considered medically untimely. Golden nicely told me I have a long time before I need to worry about that. I mention that I'm 56. She asked that her last statement be stricken from the record.

After 15 tough miles, we made camp early where I did a little laundry and washed up in the creek. As I hung my wet clothes in a nearby tree, it began to hail. I doubted they'd be dry in the morning.

Chapter 17: Lake City

Day 24 started out, hmmmm, clear and we had 10 miles to hike to get near the town of Lake City. Much of the morning involved a long trek through the high tundra of aptly named Snow Mesa. It's the middle of July and there are still pockets of snow.

As we hiked I met two more hikers, Gimpy and Gristle. They're both around 60 and live 7 miles from each other in Texas. The funny thing is, they didn't know each other until they'd met on the trail a few days earlier.

The ladies made it to the road first and quickly got a ride into town. Shockingly, it took a bit longer for the 4 guys to get a lift. Five of us with 4 packs crammed into a Kia Rodeo. Three of us sat with packs on our laps in the back seat. The ride is 17 miles downhill and you could smell the brakes overheating just a few miles into the twisted downslope. White Pine buried his head in his pack so he couldn't see. I concentrated on the sticker that warns of the vehicle's high center of gravity and rollover potential as we whipped through the turns. Our ride ended at the edge of town when the driver pulled into the local liquor store. After kissing the ground, it was just a short walk to the center of town and the local motels and hostel.

I headed for Silver Spur Motel while others all head into the hostel. After Golden received an inordinate amount of attention at the hostel, the ladies also decided to "upgrade" to a room at the Silver Spur. White Pine had no such issues and decided to stick it out where he was.

Crossing paths later at the local laundry, the ladies were intrigued that I was wearing clean, cotton clothes while feeding quarters into the dryer. Apparently I was the first thru-hiker they knew to think of mailing himself throw away clothing with the rest of the resupply package. Perhaps I'll start a trend. Despite mailing food to myself, I needed to load up at the grocery store as well. I've been constantly hungry on the trail and have lost more weight. I need to carry more food, pack weight be damned.

One night in town was enough for White Pine and he headed back out on the trail where he'd wait for the rest of The Family to catch up. The rest of us took a zero mileage day to stay in town, relax, eat and even stroll through the arts and crafts fair that closed one of the town's 3 streets.

While in town I got an update that "the boy," Matt, will be getting home from the Peace Corps a few days earlier than he had planned. In addition, I also saw that two people had been killed and over a dozen hospitalized due to lightning strikes in the higher elevations of Rocky Mountain National Park. The better part of the next 40 miles of the Colorado Trail is over 12,000 feet in elevation.

Between wanting to see Matt as soon as possible and not wanting to spend additional time in the lightning kill zone, my thoughts about slowing down went out the window. I would just work as hard as needed to stay with The Family and put in big miles. They've been a great group to hike with and I was sure they'd help me along. I'd just need to stay a safe distance from Golden when she used her umbrella during the thunderstorms. Now that I've settled into the trail name of Simba, I'd rather stay with that than get hit by lightning and have a new name like "Juice," "Twitchy," "Crispy" or "Toast."

Chapter 18: Onto the High Ground

After getting a ride from Crazy Mike back to the trailhead for the start of day 26, we were joined by Bob, trail name Bob, who was also thru-hiking. Bob started the same day that I did, but had skipped the snow section, and also had to leave the trail for a funeral.

While the day started clear, a massive thunderstorm built quickly and headed right for us. We were in a high open area and made a beeline for a small group of trees. Golden, Wildflower and I set up tents near, but not in, the clump of trees. Bob decided to just go with his raingear. The storm hit with tremendous force. Lightning was hitting all around, the wind was fierce and the rain was coming down in buckets. The only thing that kept my tent from flying away was the pack and I still weigh over 200 pounds total. After about 20 minutes the wind noise dropped just enough that I could yell, "Hey Bob, how's that rain gear working out for you?" I could only hear a partial reply, but I think I heard the words, "wish," and "tent," along with several others I won't repeat here.

Once storm went through, the temperature dropped significantly and no more storms developed. As we walked ever higher, we came across a herd of sheep being guarded by two very attentive sheep dogs. It was pretty interesting watching them work the herd.

Early afternoon we came upon a yurt where White Pine had waited out the storm. This is one of only a couple possible shelters on the entire trail. As the sky stayed clear, we all decided to risk putting in more miles. Before the day was over, we had climbed to the highest point on the trail, over 13,200 feet. Hopefully the regular afternoon thunderstorms will hold off for another day or two. I was dealing with more Achilles trouble. Hopefully just another one-day issue.

Chapter 19: Walking the Great Divide

It was cold and clear in the morning, probably about freezing.

Five minutes into the day, Bob and I found the trail blocked by two moose. They looked at us, looked at each other, then looked at us some more. The standoff lasted about 5 minutes before they decided to drop off the trail. It's a good thing as we had nowhere to go if they had decided to charge. Worst case scenario though, I was fairly sure I could outrun Bob.

We spent the entire day bouncing between 12-13,000 feet, mostly along the Continental Divide. Luckily, we caught a real break with the weather as it stayed nice and clear as the whole day was above timberline. I filled up on drinking water from the Rio Grande when it was nothing more than a bit of snowmelt. It was no problem to step across the river and keep your feet dry. There's still significant snow in the spectacular San Juan Mountains. We end up camping at 12,500 feet, highest of the entire trip. There was no doubt it was going to be a cold night.

Day 28 – Woke up to a hard freeze and an iced over tent. I was cold, but not miserable and actually slept pretty good. This might be a good time to explain White Pine's minimalist approach to camping equipment. His sleeping bag is rated for

40 degrees (mine is 23). Instead of a tent, he sleeps under a tarp. Not just any tarp, but one made out of the clear, thin plastic that is used to cover windows. The stuff that's a little thinner than plastic food wrap (think Saran Wrap). If he gets too cold, he builds a fire to stay warm. Unfortunately, when camping in tundra well above tree line, there's no wood to burn. Earlier in the trip, he actually had a Snowshoe Hare come in under the tarp to sleep by his feet, warming him a bit. There would be no rabbits or marmots joining him this night though. By 3 am, White Pine was out of his cozy tarp, doing calisthenics in an attempt to deal with the sub-freezing temperature. Survival Boot Camp lasted until first light. Thankfully he didn't need music to work out so I slept blissfully unaware of his predicament. I'm 395 miles deep into the mountains.

Chapter 20: Into Silverton

"Mountains are not Stadiums where I satisfy my ambition to achieve; they are the cathedrals where I practice my religion."
Anatoli Boukreev

After a short walk through the cloudless high tundra in the morning, the trail follows a narrow ridge between two canyons, then begins the long descent through the Weminuche Wilderness down towards the town of Silverton.

The canyon I drop into literally looked like it was out of a movie. I am not an extraordinarily religious person, but this valley felt like it was carved by God himself. I started the descent on over two dozen switchbacks . The ground was slightly less steep than a cliff, yet it's packed with wildflowers thicker than I'd ever seen in my life.

Once through the switchbacks, the drop continued steeply through a field of boulders and alongside a rushing stream of clear cold snowmelt, joined by more streams and waterfalls all along the way. Across the stream, sheer cliffs towered a thousand feet overhead. The beauty and majesty were enough to put a lump in my throat every time I looked around. I couldn't spend too much time wandering in awe however, as much of the trail is scratched into the side of a cliff where a bad step could end my trip for good. And this went on literally for miles. If you are capable of a hard hike at altitude, put Elk Creek Canyon on your bucket list. Neither words nor pictures do it justice.

There is an expression among long distance hikers; "Hike your own hike." One of the things that I thought would make my hike special would be the rare opportunity that presents itself near where Elk Creek empties into the Animas River. At this spot, you can walk out of the woods onto a train track, wave down a steam locomotive, slip the conductor $35, and ride the train into town. That was an opportunity I was not going to miss! While the others walked the last few miles into Silverton, I "rode the rails" straight out of history and into the scenic mountain village. There I proceeded to eat a half pound hamburger, then a half pound buffalo burger, along with fries and a salad while waiting for their arrival so we could eat. Tasty.

(For those of you that have a problem with me skipping a few miles of trail to ride the train; remember I will walk 99% of the possible mileage of the trail. In addition, I may have the opportunity to pick up those miles at a later date. Also, remember that saying, "Hike your own hike?" Hike your own damn hike. Oh, and I stopped a train!)

Silverton would be a quick, overnight stop to resupply, then the final stretch into Durango and completion of the Colorado Trail!

Chapter 21: The Final Stretch

As I lay in the tent I could hear the heavy footsteps of the bear as it entered the camp. It began sniffing at my tent and somehow I knew it was a matter of time before it was coming in. Silently I opened the lock blade on my pocketknife and waited. If it was a mature Grizzly, I didn't have a great chance to survive an attack, but if I could just inflict enough damage, maybe it would leave without harming anyone else. "If I save the rest of 'The Family'" I grimly thought, "that wouldn't be a bad way to check out." Just then the massive head tore through the nylon tent wall and the big Grizzly's first bite was to my shoulder….

That's when I woke up back home in Cincinnati as my stupid, stupid cat was clawing my shoulder in an attempt to wake me up. Once the cat (bear) was locked out of the room, I could reminisce in peace about what actually happened on the home stretch of the hike.

On Day 29 we still had 75 miles to go. Five of us, The Family and Gimpy, got a ride up to Molas Pass on a sunny Saturday morning. This section of trail was popular with the mountain bikers and we were passed by over 100 of them. We hit the high pass (12,500 feet) at the same time as a nasty looking thunderstorm, waited about an hour as it slid by, but ended up staying dry for another day. This made for long day as we had trouble finding a good camp site. After 20 miles walked, we caught back up with Gimpy who had himself caught up to and set up camp by Bob.

Day 30 was a tough water day. Six of us started out, loading up on water at Straight Creek, 7.5 miles into the day. The next sure water source was 22 miles distant, though we heard from a north bound hiker that there was a small supply in 15 miles. Since his trail name was Pants on Fire, I had my doubts. Each of us carried 3 liters of water, but we would need it all, and more, if we couldn't make it to water that day. The sun was out in force from sunup to sundown. Much of the trail was old Forest Service roads which let in most of the sun's power, drying us out.

The views were still tremendous, so that part stayed great. Our merry band picked up another member when a south bounder that was going to take another week to finish suddenly decided to speed up and stay with "the cool kids table." Casey was a science student and stated he wanted to work at a job that hadn't been invented yet. Hmmm, maybe he'll be a flying car mechanic.

At 7 pm, after hiking 22.5 miles in the blazing sun, we happened across the water supply and a spot to set up 7 tents. You wouldn't think people would be so excited about getting a drink of water out of a small, mossy creek, but when it's the only option, it tastes wonderful.

By day 31 things started to wind down. Gimpy and Bob took off early, but The Family only planned to hike about 16 miles, leaving 14 or so to get to the finish in Durango. We recorded the last of Golden's Monday Videos for her blog. This one involved five hikers dancing (poorly) down the trail to the relaxing strains of "We Found Love" by Rihanna. In addition, we still climbed to over 12,000 feet one last time through the La Plata Mountains. I found it hard to believe, but the views continued to get even better.

As we walked a high ridge, a look to the left provided a view that reminded me of the Smoky Mountains, but more rugged. A glance to the right gave me a view of snow touched majesty that is classic rugged Rocky Mountains. Eventually we dropped down far enough to get back into Aspen trees and camp near a "gurgling" stream.

The last day was spent on a slow drop in altitude down to around 7,000 feet. Although by most standards the scenery remained tremendous, it can't compete with the above the tree line views of the previous days. Mostly I walked alone, trying to absorb just a little more of the experience before it ended. By midafternoon, we reached a sign telling us we are done; all five members of The Family have thru-hiked the Colorado Trail. After congratulatory hugs and photos, we began walking towards Durango and its hotels, showers and brewpubs. Luckily we all quickly got a ride.

After cleaning up, The Family met up at Carver's Brewpub in downtown Durango. As promised, they provide a free glass of Colorado Trail, Nut Brown Ale to all thru hikers. The evening was spent reliving recent memories with great new friends, plates of good food and more than enough beer. The trip had been, in a word, epic; simply epic.

Back in Cincinnati and fully awake, I pulled on my running shoes and limp out to the road for a training run. I'd be back in Colorado for the race up Pike's Peak in a few short weeks. Refusing (denying) to get old is a never ending task.

"Climb the mountains and get their good tidings. Nature's peace will flow into you as sunshine flows into trees. The winds will blow their own freshness into you, and the storms their energy, while cares will drop away from you like the leaves of Autumn."

John Muir

Chapter 22: More Punishment

Three weeks later, it's like deja vu all over again. I'm standing in a valley looking up at a huge rock that I need to climb. Only this time, I know exactly what's in front of me. For the third straight year, I toe the starting line of the Pike's Peak Ascent Race.

The "Peak" is an unusual race in that you can actually see the finish from the starting line. Seeing it and getting there are two different things however. The course is 13.32 miles long, but it also climbs a total of 7,815 feet, ending at an elevation of 14,115 feet above sea level. This is a brutal race that typically takes a runner longer than a full marathon would at more normal altitudes. As an indication of its toughness, it was chosen to be the World Mountain Running Association's 2014 World Championship Race. (I would not be challenging the front-runners.)

The race is especially tough on flatlanders such as myself. Besides the unrelenting climb, there's about 20% less oxygen available than you're used to....at the start. By the time you reach the finish line, the oxygen content of the air is down by about 40%. In addition, the weather can be a tad variable. In 2013, I started the race on a sunny, 60 degree morning and broke through the tree line into a windy snowstorm.

The past two years, the race has taken me over five hours to complete; and it was not a pleasant five hours. Towards the top I had to stop and rest multiple times. It was that or fall down. During one section where the trail is etched into a cliff I repeatedly told myself to “lean left,” which was uphill. My hope was that by leaning correctly, I would merely drop onto rocks when I passed out, rather than head out into thin air. It seemed like a good plan at the time.

Standing at the start this year and staring at the finish line I had the same, “Holy shit, what the hell did I sign up for?” feeling as in past years, but it wasn’t quite as intense. While the lack of run training was worrisome, the month spent hiking at altitude gave me the confidence to know I could finish; I just didn’t know how fast (or slow) I’d be. It would be interesting to see how much the toughened legs and extra (or are they just bigger?) red blood cells helped.

It’s clear and warm at 7:30 am when the gun fires and about 1,100 of us start jogging through the town of Manitou Springs. Another 700 or so “elite” runners started at 7 am. The first mile or so on roads thins the crowd, but it is still a clog at the start of the trail which, for the most part, is single file. For the first several miles there is a combination of a slow jog on the flatter sections (under a 10% grade) and walking the steeper sections.

By the time I reach the water station at Barr Camp, (7.6 miles and 4,000 feet of climb) I had been going for a bit over 2 hours. The time is a few minutes faster than in previous years, but I feel much better. At tree line (10 miles and 5,700 feet of climb) I’m still just barely ahead of my earlier attempts.

Above tree line is where things get tough. In years past, the final 3.1 miles (5K) had taken me nearly 2 hours. This is where hiking 500 miles at altitude begins to make a real difference. With no 30 pound pack on my back and plenty of extra (or are they giant?) red blood cells to deliver fuel and oxygen to the leg muscles, there is no need to stop, or for that matter, even slow down dramatically. I grind up the final stretch, passing dozens of competitors as I go. The weather remains clear with temperatures in the 50s. I finish the race, actually feeling good, at 4:44:44, nearly a half hour faster than my previous best time this century. My first thought on finishing is, "Crap, I'll have to hike the entire Colorado Trail again next year to have any chance to improve my time much more." Perhaps the glass is still half empty.

After a short visit with my brother Dan in Denver, it is time to head out. As I drive away, I still haven't decided whether to head east, back home, or west to deal with those few miles of the Colorado Trail I had skipped to ride the train into Silverton. I guess I'll see which way I turn when I get to I-70.

Chapter 23: How About It?

"We are now in the mountains and they are in us, kindling enthusiasm, making every nerve quiver, filling every pore and cell of us."

John Muir

Well, it's almost time to put down the book and start planning your own epic adventure on the Colorado Trail. If you still need more information to decide whether to take on the challenge of the Trail, look no further than www.coloradotrail.org. The site covers most any question you might have and they responded quickly when I emailed with specific inquiries. In addition, the site also sells guides that you'll want to have.

The Colorado Trail Guidebook is nearly 300 pages of information about the trail, mountains, flora and fauna, as well as resupply towns. This is a great planning tool that you don't want to be without.

The Colorado Trail Databook puts nearly all the information that you'll need while actually on the trail into an easy to follow 4 ounce package. Every intersection, water source, access point and major point of interest is pinpointed along with simplified maps of the trail. Many, but not all, campsites are listed as well. This little book was indispensable while I was in the mountains

The Colorado Trail Map Book provides detailed maps of every section of the trail along with 1,200 GPS waypoints. If you're into maps, this is the book for you. However, if the simple maps of the Databook are good enough and you just wanting waypoints to load into your GPS, try www.bearcreeksurvey.com. The same waypoints are downloadable from there in a .gpx format that most GPS receivers can understand.

If you are seriously considering hiking the Colorado Trail, or any long trail for that matter; I do have one other book recommendation for you. Appalachian Trials was written by AT thru-hiker Zach Davis and is not your typical trail journal/book. The work delves into the psychology of long distance hiking; why so many people fail to complete their hike and ideas on how to better put the odds in your favor. I used several of his suggestions myself and they helped out when times got hard. On top of that, it is well written and an enjoyable read.

I hope this book has increased your interest in hiking the Colorado Trail. Make no mistake though, the hiking is tough. In talking with Golden about it, she felt that between the altitude and the lack of support facilities on or near the trail, the CT is actually a more difficult hike than the AT. However, the time investment is doable for many and the payoff is immense. The scenery was nothing short of spectacular, day after day, after day. Wildlife was abundant. The wildflowers were amazing and constant. The feeling of accomplishment, not just at the finish, but throughout the hike was second to none.

If you can't spare the four to six weeks required to thru-hike, pick a section and try it out. Odds are you'll be back the next year to knock off another section. In just a few years, you'll have successfully and completely hiked "the most beautiful long trail in the world."

Good luck.

Chapter 24: My Gear

While I'm certainly no backpacking gear expert, I did spend quite a bit of time researching, testing and living with the gear I used on the trail. It may have been just luck, but all my gear worked, for the most part, flawlessly. In case you are interested, here's what I brought.

Pack – Osprey Exos 58, size large. The pack weighs only 2 lb, 12 ounce and has a 61 liter volume. It was comfortable handling my 30-35 pound load, but I believe that is near the top end of the range for the pack.

Tent – Big Agnes Copper Spur UL 1 which only tips the scale at 2lb, 3 ounce, is self standing and was big enough that, at 6 ft, 3 inches, I didn't feel overly cramped. It set up quick and held up to some significant storms. Ventilation could have been better, but it wasn't bad. For another 4.5 ounces, I got the footprint as well.

Sleeping Bag – Sierra Designs Zissou 23 with "DriDown." The bag weighs 2 lb, 3 ounce in long. The EN comfort rating is 34 degrees for women and 23 for men. When combined with a silk liner (4.5 ounce), I could sleep comfortably to around 30 degrees before needing to wear my fleece. Long underwear would have helped, had I brought any. I never "wet the bag" to test the DriDown, though it stayed warm when damp from condensation.

Pad - Therm-a-Rest Neo-Air. This was an older version that weighs 12 ounces. I was worried it might spring a leak, but it held up just fine.

Cooking kit - GSI Outdoors Pinnacle Soloist Cookset. The pot, lid, cup and a foldable spork weigh in at just under 10 ounces (leave the storage sack at home). The no name, folding canister stove fits inside the pot, and weighs 4 ounces. My stove cost less than 6 bucks yet nothing, including the built-in igniter, ever failed. Google "cheap camping stove" and it should be at the top of the list. A small gas canister also fits in the pot, weighs 8 ounces full, and lasted me five days or more when heating water for instant oatmeal in the morning and a wholesome freeze-dried dinner at night.

Water Filter/Storage – Sawyer Mini Filter with a one liter and three liter squeeze bag. I also used a small "bottled water" bottle to dip in the creeks to fill the squeeze bottles. Filtered water was kept in a one liter Nalgene bottle (the soft ones are lighter) and a one liter Gatorade bottle (lighter still). I also brought some chlorine dioxide tablets for back up. Everything together, except the actual water, weighed in at 12 ounces.

Small "essentials" – Petzl Tikka Plus headlamp weighed 4 oz including the one set of lithium batteries that lasted the entire trip. Small folding knife at 2 oz. Plastic shovel at 2 oz. Twenty five feet of rope to hang food at 3 oz. Pack rain cover at 4 oz. Colorado Trail travel size Databook (and pen) at 4 oz. Small first aid kit at 4 oz. which included a few Band-Aids, a gauze pad, tape, alcohol pads, anti-bacterial pads, sting relief pad, blister covers and a small anti-friction stick.

Smaller "essentials" – compass, mini camera tripod, 3 feet of duct tape, small spray bottle of Deet insect repellent, 2 lighters (never used), bug head net (never used), small multi-tool, small pepper spray (to irritate bears…never used), sleeping pad repair kit (never used), sewing needle (never used) and Neo-Air inflatable seat (which sprung a leak). Everything together weighed 12 oz.

Toiletries – Toilet paper, sanitizer, contact lens solution, case and mirror, toothbrush and paste, Aleve, aspirin, Advil PM, Imodium (never used), Wet Ones hand/face wipes and sunscreen. Total weight of 16 oz.

Clothing – Typically I was wearing North Face nylon zip off pants/shorts, Smartwool lightweight t-shirt, short wool socks, nylon ball cap and Exofficio underwear. Boxers or briefs? It depends. Spares in the pack were one pair of underwear, two pair of socks, lightweight Columbia nylon pants, a 100 weight Columbia fleece pullover, Under Armor t-shirt, cheap rain pants, Outdoor Research packable rain jacket, nylon gloves and watchman's cap. Crammed, as most items were, in Ziploc bags, the extra clothes weighed 3 lbs, 2 oz. I never suffered from a lack of clothes, but at one time or another, I did use every item of extra clothing.

Shoes - I read somewhere that an extra pound of weight on your feet is like carrying five extra pounds in your pack. This may or may not be accurate, but for me, heavy boots are a significant drag on my ability to hike long distances. I went fairly lightweight by wearing waterproof trail running shoes, specifically Saucony Xodus GTX. Even with the neuroma inserts the size 13 pair weighed just over 2 lbs, and held up admirably. In the pack was a 1lb, 6 oz pair of "camp" sandals. Because the shoes were comfortable and the inserts helped my feet feel better, I rarely wore the sandals. Eventually they were left at Lake City in an attempt to lighten the pack for the final push.

Electronics – This is where I might have gone a tad overboard. The Spot Satellite Messenger weighed 5oz. I used it on a daily basis to let friend(s) and family know where I was and that I was OK. Luckily I never had to try the other buttons that told them I was lost, had a shattered pelvis or lost a fight with a bear.

The Garmin Etrex 20 GPS weighs 5 oz and was extremely useful in keeping me headed in the right direction when the trail was covered with snow. Beyond that, it confirmed that I was still on the correct trail a couple times, but would not have been necessary had I been traveling after more of the snow had melted.

My IPhone weighed 6 oz, was used as a back up camera and allowed "texts and talk," along with email and internet when I was in or near towns. The IPad Mini, at 14 oz, did everything the phone did, except phone calls, in a larger, easier to use size. In addition, the piece also provided reading material and served as a notepad to write down my thoughts at the end of the day.

My dedicated camera was a Canon SX 160 that weighed 10 oz. While it took some great shots, the pictures from the IPhone look, in many instances, as good or better.

Of course with this much in the way of electronics, there has to be charging cords, cords to download photos from the camera to the IPad, extra batteries and a small solar charger. That "bag o' stuff" tipped the scales at another 10 oz. In total, while I was "getting away from it all," I carried over 3 lbs of gizmos.

Add everything up and my pack, including the sandals I later abandoned, started out at just over 21 pounds, plus food and water. Filling the 2 water bottles added 4 lbs. The food I packed weighed approximately 22 oz per day, and it wasn't enough. However, four days' worth would bring the total weight of my pack to around 31 lbs.

There are ways to lower this weight, and many easy ways to increase it, but other than needing a bit more food, I felt like I had all the equipment necessary to stay comfortable on the trail under normal circumstances.

Final Travel Detail

Mileage based on Colorado Trail Databook.

Day	Date	Miles	Total Miles From Start	Segment	Comments
1	6/21	16.8	16.8	1	Day hike segment #1
2	6/22	11.5	28.3	2	Day hike segment #2
3	6/23	15.5	43.8	3-4	Camp in Lost Creek Wilderness area. Carry 5 days food
4	6/24	20.6	64.4	4-5	Camp by Rock Creek
5	6/25	10.4	74.8	5-6	Camp by Guernsey Creek

6	6/26	16.6	91.4	6	Camp by Swan River
7	6/27	13	104.4	6	Bus to Frisco/ Breckenridge Fuel at Mt Outfitters in Breckenridge Stayed at Snowshoe Motel
8	6/28	14.4	118.8	7-8	Slack pack Segment 7 + distance to Copper Mountain Resort
9	6/29	0	118.8	8	Zero in Frisco
10	6/30	14.2	133	8	Camp by Cataract Creek. Carry 5 days food

11	7/1	20.5	153.5	8-9	Camp near ponds
12	7/2	15.8	169.3	11	Stayed w brothers in Leadville. Fuel and supply package at Twin Lakes
13	7/3	11.4	180.7	11	Slack pack
14	7/4	16.5	197.2	11-12	Camp by Pine Creek
15	7/5	14.6	211.8	12-13	Camp by Silver Creek
16	7/6	21.3	233.5	13-14	Dry camp on knoll above Chalk Creek
17	7/7	19	252.5	14	Stay in Salida

18	7/8	0	252.5	14	Supply Box @ Post Office. 6 days food. Fuel at Salida Mt Sports
19	7/9	14.3	266.8	15	Slack pack
20	7/10	22.1	288.9	16-17	Camp by Baldy Lake
21	7/11	22.7	311.6	17-18	Camp .2 mile past Los Creek
22	7/12	19.9	331.5	18-20	Camp near Cochetopa Creek
23	7/13	15.1	346.6	20-21	Camp by Mineral Creek
24	7/14	10.8	357.4	21	Lake City
25	7/15	0	357.4	21	Supply box @ Post Office. 4 days food. Fuel @ The Sportsman

26	**7/16**	**18.6**	**376**	**22-23**	**Camp near small stream**
27	7/17	19.8	395.8	23-24	Camp on tundra near small pond
28	7/18	9.8	405.6	24	Train into Silverton Resupply @ grocery, 4.5 days. Fuel @ Outdoor World
29	7/19	21	431.6	25	Camp by Celebration Lake
30	7/20	22.6	454.2	26-27	Camp near small seepage
31	7/21	16	470.2	27-28	Camp by Junction Creek
32	7/22	14.4	484.6	28	Complete!

Acknowledgements

While heading out to solo thru-hike a long trail is, by definition, a solitary venture, I had the benefit of quite a bit of help both before and during the trip. Some probably had no idea they were helping me down the path to this epic adventure, but I'd like to thank them regardless.

I did quite a bit of car camping and canoe camping through my life, but had not been backpacking in nearly 25 years when an old friend and former co-worker Bill Mowery invited me along on a late fall trip to a nearby state forest a few years ago. Between the scenery, camaraderie and the simple joy of sipping a flask by the campfire, I was hooked.

Despite being half my age, Brittney Graham invited me to try skydiving with her and teamed up with me to compete in my first triathlon in decades. She helped me to realize that I'm not too old to get out of my comfort zone or to think about big adventures.

When I wondered about the commitment to hike 500 miles and camp out for 5 weeks, I just thought of my boy, Matt. His voluntary obligation to the Peace Corps of spending over two years in China was dramatically more than the level of commitment I would need. If he could do that, I could certainly put up with any inconveniences that I'd encounter along the way.

My brother Dan went above and beyond to assist me in this endeavor. His home became my base of operations; he drove me all over the state, hiked with me and encouraged me the entire way. The hike was significantly easier because of his efforts. When he and another brother (Bob) met me near Twin Lakes, it was a great boost when the hike was starting to drag. In addition, Bob put his English degree to work helping me edit this work.

My ex-wife Michelle also encouraged me in this adventure, and not just because it got me out of town. While I was hiking she handled the posting of my "from the trail" updates. Through everything she has remained a true friend.

And then there's The Family. There is nothing quite like a shared adventure to bring people together in a hurry. From the first offer of green eggs and ham I knew I was with a group that would support each other and enjoy each other's company. While no one needed help to finish, I'm sure it would have been there if needed. Golden, Wildflower, White Pine and Casey; you were terrific hiking partners.

Sincere thanks to all of you.

Printed in the USA
CPSIA information can be obtained
at www.ICGtesting.com
LVHW012254050824
787460LV00036B/738